The Truth

Florian Zeller is a French novelist and playwright. He won the prestigious Prix Interallié in 2004 for his third novel, *Fascination of Evil*. His plays include *L'Autre, Le Manège, Si tu mourais*, nominated for a Globe de Cristal, *Elle t'attend* and *La Vérité*. *La Mère* (*The Mother*, Molière Award for Best Play in 2011) and *Le Père* (*The Father*, Molière Award for Best Play in 2014, starring Robert Hirsch and Isabelle Gelinas (Molière Awards for Best Actor and Actress, Prix du Brigadier in 2015). *Une Heure de tranquillité* (*A Bit of Peace and Quiet*), opened with Fabrice Luchini, and has since been adapted for the screen, directed by Patrice Leconte. *Le Mensonge* (*The Lie*) was staged in 2015 starring Pierre Arditi and Evelyne Bouix and *L'Envers du décor* opened in January 2016 at the Théâtre de Paris starring Daniel Auteuil.

Christopher Hampton was born in the Azores in 1946. He wrote his first play, *When Did You Last See My Mother?*, at the age of eighteen. Since then, his plays have included *The Philanthropist, Savages, Tales from Hollywood, Les Liaisons Dangereuses, White Chameleon, The Talking Cure* and *Appomattox*. He has translated plays by Ibsen, Molière, von Horváth, Chekhov and Yasmina Reza (including '*Art*', *Life × 3*, and *The God of Carnage*). His television work includes adaptations of *The History Man* and *Hotel du Lac*. His screenplays include *The Honorary Consul, The Good Father, Dangerous Liaisons, Mary Reilly, Total Eclipse, The Quiet American, Atonement, Cheri, A Dangerous Method, Carrington, The Secret Agent* and *Imagining Argentina*, the last three of which he also directed.

FLORIAN ZELLER

The Truth

translated by
CHRISTOPHER HAMPTON

FABER & FABER

First published in 2016
by Faber and Faber Limited
The Bindery, 51 Hatton Garden
London EC1N 8HN

Typeset by Country Setting, Kingsdown, Kent CT14 8ES
Printed in England by CPI Bookmarque, Croydon, Surrey

A CIP record for this book
is available from the British Library

ISBN 978-0-571-32744-7

Printed and bound in the UK on FSC® certified paper in line with our continuing
commitment to ethical business practices, sustainability and the environment.
For further information see faber.co.uk/environmental-policy

A lie is only a sin if it does harm. When it does good, it's a very great virtue. So be ever more virtuous. You have to lie like the devil, not tentatively, not provisionally, but boldly and constantly. Lie, my friends, lie, when the time comes, I'll do the same for you.

Voltaire

As you are my best and oldest friend and, in the present instance, my host, I decided to take this opportunity to tell your wife how beautiful she was.

Pinter, *Betrayal*

The Truth, in this translation by Christopher Hampton, was first presented in association with Theatre Royal Bath Productions at the Menier Chocolate Factory, London, on 10 March 2016. The cast, in order of appearance, was as follows:

Michel Alexander Hanson
Alice Frances O'Connor
Laurence Tanya Franks
Paul Robert Portal

Direction Lindsay Posner
Design Lizzie Clachan
Lighting Howard Harrison
Sound Gregory Clarke
Original Music Matthew Scott
Voice and Dialect Coach Penny Dyer
Associate Director Lisa Blair

This production transferred to Wyndham's Theatre, London, on 22 June 2016.

La Vérité in its original French production opened at the Théâtre Montparnasse, Paris, on 23 September 2011, with Pierre Arditi, Fanny Cottençon, Christine Millet and Patrice Kerbrat, who also directed.

Characters

Michel

Laurence

Paul

Alice

Simple sets.
The capacity to move very swiftly
from one to another.

THE TRUTH

THE ADVANTAGES OF CONCEALING IT,
THE DRAWBACKS TO REVEALING IT

ONE
THE RENDEZVOUS

Michel and Alice. A room. They've just made love.
Longish pause. Then he starts looking for his things and
it's clear he's getting ready to leave.

Alice I adore making love to you.

Michel is elsewhere.

Michel You do?

Alice Yes, I adore it. But you know what I love best?

Michel What?

Alice You know what I love best?

Michel No. You haven't seen my socks, have you?
They've vanished.

Alice It's when you cuddle up against me for a nice long
time . . . After making love . . . You hardly ever do it.
You're always getting ready to leave.

Michel Me?

Alice Yes. You. You're always in a hurry.

Michel What makes you say that?

Alice Now, for example, you have to go . . .

It's as if Michel has been caught in flagrante.

Michel What?

Alice Am I wrong?

Michel I'm late, Alice.

Pause.

I'm sorry. It's an important meeting . . .

Alice I know.

Michel kisses her. Then he gets out of bed to get dressed. She takes a cigarette, but doesn't light it. Pause. Michel is searching for a soothing phrase.

Michel And your husband, everything all right?

Alice What?

Michel How is he?

Alice How's who?

Michel You know, Paul.

Alice Oh . . . all right. That's to say, as you well know . . . he's still looking for work.

Michel Poor old sod.

Alice Yes, but you've seen him recently, haven't you?

Michel What? Oh, yes. We played tennis last week.

Alice Yes, that's what he said.

Michel But I haven't seen him since. I've tried to call him several times. Yesterday, day before. But he didn't answer. I was worried.

Alice Why did you want to speak to him?

Michel To ask him how he was. You know, I still can't get over the way the bastards threw him out. Those people have no decency, really. No, it's true: they take you, they use you up and throw you away . . . It's disgusting. Don't you think?

Alice Erm . . .

Michel People don't go in for ethics any more. Ethics are a thing of the past. Makes me sick!

Short pause.

But he told me about an opening for some . . .

Alice Yes, that's right. A Swedish firm. He saw them again yesterday.

Michel And?

Alice The interview went well. They're going to let him know soon.

Michel Good . . . I thought he seemed rather gloomy the other day. Don't you think? I just hope he finds something soon . . .

Alice Do you mind changing the subject?

Michel Why?

Alice It makes me feel uncomfortable . . .

Michel I don't see why.

Alice Because we talk about him all the time.

Michel (*trying to put things in perspective*) All the time, all the time . . .

Alice Well, we do, Michel . . . we hardly talk about anything else.

Michel It's understandable, isn't it? He's one of my best friends . . . He's just lost his job. I'm entitled to worry about him, don't you think?

Alice Yes, but it makes me feel guilty . . .

Michel (*on his high horse*) Oh, no, Alice. Not that . . . Not between us.

Alice (*startled*) Not what?

Michel Anything you like, but not guilt. I hate that feeling.

Alice You hate all feelings.

Michel (*amused*) Me? I hate all feelings? Me?

Alice Yes.

Michel I hate all feelings?

Alice Yes.

Michel Is that a criticism?

Alice It's an observation.

Michel An observation?

Alice An objective observation.

Michel (*forced laugh*) I 'hate all feelings' is an objective observation?

Alice Entirely.

Michel You think I'm heartless, is that it?

   Pause. No reply.

She thinks I'm heartless . . . let me remind you I've been diagnosed with tachycardia.

Alice So?

Michel So? Proves I have a heart.

Alice Proves nothing of the sort.

Michel I'm sorry, it proves I have a heart. It even proves that it's beating. Beating too fast, as it turns out.

Alice I meant something different, as you very well know.

Michel No, I don't know. What are you trying to tell me?

Alice How long have we been seeing each other?

Michel Us?

Alice Yes. How long?

Michel Mm? Six months . . . Something like that.

He looks at her. No reaction. Has he got the dates wrong?

(*Hesitantly.*) Seven months . . . Between four and eight months. More or less.

Alice And you've never felt guilty?

Michel About what?

Alice Your wife. For example.

Michel Mm? Yes. A bit.

Alice Not noticeably.

Michel It's just I find guilt so useless.

Alice Lucky man.

He checks his watch.

Michel You haven't seen my sock?

Alice No.

Michel The right one . . .

She lights her cigarette, which she's been playing with all this time. She's thinking. He notices.

Something wrong?

Alice It's all right. It's just . . .

Michel Just what?

Alice No, nothing.

Pause.

Actually, this isn't working for me.

Michel What isn't?

Alice It isn't working for me at all. Seeing each other like this. Between two meetings. You realise we've never spent a single night together? In six months . . .

Michel I know.

Alice Don't you feel the lack?

Michel What?

Alice Don't you feel the lack?

Michel Of course . . . but we have no choice, Alice.

Alice I don't see why not.

Michel You don't see why not?

Alice No.

Michel You don't see why we have no choice?

Alice No.

Michel You are married, let me remind you.

Alice What's that supposed to mean? You're married as well.

Michel It's not the same for me.

Alice It's not the same?

Michel Not at all. I'm sorry, it's not at all the same thing.

Alice Oh?

Michel No. Not at all. I mean, not at all!

Alice And in what way is it not the same thing?

Michel What?

Alice In what way is it not the same thing?

Short hesitation.

Michel What?

Alice We're both married, Michel.

Michel Yes, but I, Alice, I was prepared to . . . to . . .

Alice To what?

Michel You know very well. You're the one who wanted us to stay in this holding pattern . . . Isn't that right?

Alice We never really discussed it.

Michel Well, I would have been prepared to . . .

Alice You never told me that, Michel.

Michel What! It was always implied, Alice. Subtext. If you don't know how to read subtext . . .

Pause.

Alice In any case, this isn't working for me. We can't go on like this . . .

Michel We have no choice, Alice . . .

Alice You're wrong. There's always a choice.

Michel All right, what are you suggesting?

Alice We could go away somewhere . . . For the weekend.

He finally finds his sock.

Michel Ah. It was under the bed.

Alice So? What do you think?

Michel About what?

Alice About going away together.

Michel You want us to spend a weekend together?

Alice Yes.

Michel How long a weekend?

Alice What do you think? . . .

Michel (*uncomfortable*) Two days?

Alice Yes. You know, I really can't do these afternoons any more.

Michel But where could we go?

Alice I don't know. Some other hotel. Somewhere else. I can't stand it here any more. The other day, when I was passing through reception, that creep was looking at me in a sort of . . . It was . . .

Michel What creep?

Alice That creep at reception. He was looking at me as if I was . . . I don't know, as if I was a tart. The way he was looking at me, it was like spitting in my face.

Michel Surely not. You were imagining it.

Alice No, I promise you. I could tell he was saying to himself, 'Like a bit of that, do you? Having a good time in a hotel room with your lovers . . .'

Michel With your lovers? What do you mean, your lovers?

Alice I'm telling you what I picked up from the way he was looking at me.

Michel But why did you say 'with your lovers'?

Alice What?

Michel Why 'with your lovers'?

Alice I don't understand the question . . .

Michel (*getting annoyed*) You just told me he was saying to himself you liked having a good time with your lovers . . . He's never seen you with anyone else, has he? He's never seen you with anyone other than me, has he? So why with your lovers . . . ?

Alice Why don't you listen to what I'm telling you instead of getting annoyed?

Michel I'm listening, but I don't understand why you're saying 'with your lovers'.

Alice To try to convey to you how uncomfortable the way he was looking at me made me.

Pause.

Michel (*calmly*) If that's the problem, we can easily meet in a different hotel . . . I mean, we don't have to go off for a weekend together. Especially a two-day weekend . . . It'd be a bit suspicious, don't you think, as far as . . . ?

Alice You don't understand.

Michel What?

Alice You don't understand.

Michel I understand completely.

Pause.

What don't I understand?

Alice You don't understand what I'm trying to say.

Michel Well then, say it, don't just try.

Alice I wanted us to be able to spend a little more time together. Do you understand? We see each other once a week . . . In a hotel room . . . We sleep together. Then you disappear . . .

While she's speaking, he's taken a discreet glance at his watch.

See.

Michel What?

Alice I'm talking to you and all you're thinking about is leaving.

Michel No, I'm not . . .

Alice Yes, you are.

Michel I already told you I was late, Alice. Don't be angry with me . . . It's this meeting . . .

Alice What about me?

Michel You're very important as well.

Alice But not as important as this meeting . . .

Michel You're far more important than this meeting. Except you don't start in half an hour . . .

Pause.

Alice Anyway, I don't know why I'm talking to you about going away for the weekend . . . It's idiotic.

Michel No, it's not idiotic . . . but it's a bit risky. Let me remind you, we're both married. Especially you. I mean, what I mean is, you're married to my best friend . . .

Alice Yes . . .

Michel Yes . . .

Pause.

Alice I think it'd be best for us to stop, Michel.

Michel To stop? You mean . . .

Alice Seeing each other. I think it'd be best.

Michel Why do you say that? Alice . . .

Alice I think it would be best.

Michel You want us to stop seeing each other?

Alice I'm tired of the lies. I'm tired of these sessions . . . It doesn't seem to make sense any more.

Michel But . . . sense? Why look for sense in everything? We have good times, don't we?

Alice No.

Michel You don't think so?

Alice I'm telling you, it isn't working for me . . .

Michel But . . .

Panic. He looks groggy.

Perhaps you're right, after all . . .

Alice I think so, yes . . .

Michel Yes. The more I think about it, the more right you seem.

Alice I think it would be the best idea . . .

Michel Yes, you're right, we ought to go away for a weekend. Somewhere or other. You've convinced me . . . It's true, we only see each other to . . . I mean, it's always between two meetings . . . We need to see each other a bit more . . . To share something a bit more . . . In short, I agree with you.

Alice Michel . . .

Michel What?

Alice Were you listening to what I just said?

Michel Yes, but I don't agree.

Alice It's true, we never see each other . . .

Michel It's not true. I'll prove it: what are you doing this afternoon?

Alice What?

Michel Aren't you working?

Alice I have patients from four o'clock on . . . Why?

Michel Kiss me.

Alice No. Go to your meeting.

Michel What meeting?

Alice Yours.

Michel takes out his telephone.

What are you doing?

Michel Saying sorry.

Alice What? What for?

Michel I've been inconsiderate to you. You're quite right to react like this . . . But I don't want to lose you. So, get your calendar and give me a date during the week . . .

Alice To do what?

Michel I'll take you somewhere.

Alice Where?

Michel What's it matter? You realise that in six months we've never spent a single night together?

Alice Yes, I realise.

Michel (*turning the tables on her*) Don't you feel the lack?

Alice (*amused*) Yes, I do.

Michel See.

Alice So what are you suggesting?

Michel dials a number on his mobile.

Michel Give me a date during the week . . . And if you have other meetings during the day, do what I'm doing: cancel them. (*To the telephone.*) Hello? Guillon? It's me.

Alice What are you doing?

Michel Yes. Listen, I'm really sorry, I don't think I'm going to be able to make the meeting . . . I know. I've come down with some little virus . . . I won't be able to come. No. I'm afraid I'm going to have to spend the rest of the day in bed . . .

She smiles. Blackout.

TWO
TIGHTROPE-WALKING

Laurence and Michel's house. That evening. He's reading the newspaper.

Laurence Your meeting go well?

Michel What? It was difficult . . . I'm knackered. But it went well.

Laurence Was it those clients from Bordeaux?

Michel Yes.

Laurence And?

Michel And nothing. It was a preliminary meeting. We haven't finalised anything.

Laurence Was Guillon there?

Michel Guillon?

Laurence Your partner.

Michel Yes, yes, thank you, I know who Guillon is . . .

Laurence Was he at the meeting?

Michel Yes. Why?

Laurence Nothing.

Pause.

Michel No, we haven't finalised anything. It was just a preliminary meeting . . . there'll have to be another one . . . In fact . . . there is another meeting . . . Next week . . . In Bordeaux.

Laurence You're going to Bordeaux?

Michel What? Yes, looks like it . . . To finalise things.

Laurence Next week? You haven't forgotten Isabelle's private view is on Wednesday . . .

Michel What? Already? You told me it was in three weeks' time!

Laurence Michel . . .

Michel What?

Laurence I never said that!

Michel I'm sorry. You told me it was in three weeks!

Laurence Three weeks ago, perhaps.

Michel Oh, God . . . Wednesday? This coming Wednesday?

Laurence I promised we'd go.

Michel I can't understand why your daughter persists with this modern art.

Laurence Your daughter as well, may I remind you? She persists because she's very talented.

Michel Talented? Laurence, it's an exhibition of soiled underwear.

Laurence With added paint.

Michel Ah yes, true, I'd forgotten. That makes all the difference.

Laurence In any case, the private view is on Wednesday. When are you supposed to be going?

Michel You mean to Bordeaux?

Laurence Yes.

Michel Thursday, I think. I'll check . . .

Pause.

It's just to finalise things.

Pause. He goes back to his newspaper.

How was your day?

Laurence No teaching today.

Michel Oh?

Laurence No. Because of the strike . . . The whole school's closed down . . . I went to the hairdresser's. Didn't you notice?

Michel Notice what?

Laurence I had it dyed blonde . . .

Michel lifts his head from the newspaper to check it isn't true.

Michel Very funny.

Laurence I went to the shopping centre. After the hairdresser's . . . Bought a few things.

Michel As you do when you're on strike.

Laurence Yes. And guess who I met in the shopping centre?

Michel Wonderful, I must say, your spirit of dissent.

Laurence Mm? Guess who I met?

Michel Who?

Laurence Guillon.

Michel lifts his head from his newspaper.

Michel Guillon?

Laurence Your partner.

Michel (*hesitantly*) What the hell was he doing at the shopping centre?

Laurence I met him just in front. In the street . . . By chance. He was getting into a taxi.

Michel Was he?

Laurence Yes. And he asked me about you. He wanted to know if you were feeling better . . .

Michel Me?

Laurence Yes.

Michel (*embarrassed smile*) What's all this about?

Laurence I was about to ask you the same question . . .

Michel (*changing the subject*) Shall I open a bottle of wine? Fancy a drop? I think I've got one last . . .

Laurence He told me you'd missed the meeting.

Michel Me?

Laurence Yes. You told him you were ill . . .

Michel Is that what he said? Guillon? Bloody Guillon . . . Guillon's always been a bit weird, you know that. Did

I tell you, he got himself discharged from the military by pretending to be insane? I've always thought there wasn't a great deal of pretence involved, if you follow my meaning . . .

Laurence Michel.

Michel Yes, darling?

Laurence Why are you lying to me?

Michel Me?

Laurence (*calmly*) Yes. Why are you lying to me?

Michel I'm not lying to you.

Laurence You told Guillon you were going to spend the rest of the day in bed. I want to know with whom.

Michel decides attack is the best defence.

Michel You want to know with whom . . . Listen to yourself! I mean, just listen to yourself! Can't you see how you're twisting the situation? 'With whom' . . . Have you any idea what you're implying? Honestly, I'm shocked at you making these insinuations. Utterly. Shocked. After twenty years of marriage . . . Who do you take me for? Someone who'd cancel a meeting without a good reason? To see another woman on the sly? Because that's what you're implying, unless I'm much mistaken. These are serious matters we're discussing, Laurence. Matters which are completely beyond you.

Laurence Well, then, explain them to me.

Michel What use would that be? You've already made up your mind.

Laurence No, I haven't . . .

Michel Yes, you have! You bump into God knows who in the street and . . .

Laurence Your partner.

Michel (*making a meal of it*) Yes, Guillon is my partner!
That's right! Absolutely! What of it? Is it a problem?
What do you want? You want me to disown him? You
want me to pretend I don't know him? You want me to
report him to the Inland Revenue? Guillon's my partner
and, whatever you think of him, I must tell you he's an
extremely good partner. I see absolutely no reason to be
ashamed of him.

　Pause.

Laurence Is that it? Are you done?

Michel Yes.

Laurence Listen, you're a grown-up, I have no intention
of spying on you in any way . . . But you must admit it's
quite painful for me to find out you've been lying to me.

Michel You don't trust me? Laurence . . . Is that what
you're trying to tell me? That's a hard thing to take after
living together for twenty years . . . It's hard, believe me.

Laurence So what did you do this afternoon?

Michel I went to see Paul.

Laurence Paul?

Michel My best friend.

Laurence Thanks, yes, I know who Paul is.

Michel Only I couldn't tell Guillon I was missing the
meeting because my best friend wasn't feeling well! I just
couldn't. That's why I told him *I* was ill . . . So there's
really no need to go making insinuations . . .

Laurence What's the matter with him?

Michel Who?

Laurence Paul.

Michel What? He wasn't feeling well. Not at all well . . . He called me around lunchtime. He looked terrible. Even on the phone. He was in a bad way. A really bad way . . . He wanted to talk . . . I could tell it was urgent . . . So I cancelled the meeting and spent the afternoon with him.

Laurence But what's the matter with him?

Michel Paul? You're asking me what's the matter with him?

Laurence Yes.

Michel Let me remind you, he's unemployed.

Laurence I know he is . . .

Michel Let me remind you he was fired three weeks ago! Overnight! Poor old sod . . . You know, I still can't get over the way the bastards threw him out. Those people have no decency, really. No, it's true: they take you, they use you up and throw you away . . . It's disgusting, don't you think?

Pause.

Anyway. He was depressed.

Laurence But I thought he had an opening for some . . .

Michel Yes, a Swedish firm. He had an interview yesterday.

Laurence Did it go badly?

Michel What? No. It went well. And they told him they'd let him know next week.

Laurence Oh, yes? That's good.

Michel Yes.

Laurence So why is he depressed?

Michel What? It's not only because of his work. It's . . . It's lots of things . . . Anyway, I prefer not to go into details.

Laurence Is it because of Alice?

Michel Excuse me?

Laurence Is it because of Alice?

Michel What do you mean, because of Alice?

Laurence His wife.

Michel No, no! How could you imagine such a thing?

Laurence I'm just asking, that's all.

Michel No, no! Really, Laurence . . . His wife? You think his wife is cheating on him? Cheating on Paul? When he's unemployed? No . . . And with one of his best friends!

Laurence What did you say?

Michel What?

Laurence What did you just say?

Michel Nothing. All I meant to say was that would be impossible. For a woman like Alice . . . (*He takes up his old refrain.*) You know, I still can't get over the way the bastards threw him out . . . Those people have no decency, really. No, it's true: they take you, they use you up and throw you away . . .

   Pause.

Laurence Are you seeing each other tomorrow?

Michel (*anxious*) Who?

Laurence You and Paul.

Michel (*relieved*) Oh . . . No. We were going to play tennis, but he cancelled it. We're playing on Monday.

Laurence Ah.

Pause. She seems odd.

Michel What is it?

Laurence Nothing.

Pause.

Michel So. Shall I open a bottle? I've a Petit Chablis, looks pretty good . . .

Laurence You know who rang a while ago?

Michel Where? Here?

Laurence Yes.

Michel No. Who?

Laurence Paul.

Michel (*going pale*) You what?

Laurence Yes. This afternoon. When you were supposed to be with him. He rang here.

Michel Here? You mean . . .

Laurence Yes. On the landline.

Michel Paul never rings on the landline.

Laurence He was looking for you. Your mobile was off, you weren't in the office . . . So he thought you might be here . . . Anyway, he called.

Michel But when? I mean, what time? I mean, was it before or after we saw each other?

Laurence You didn't see him, Michel.

Michel Laurence . . .

Laurence What?

Michel Don't play these games with me . . .

Laurence That's exactly what I was going to say.

Michel Laurence . . .

Laurence What?

Michel (*his inspiration failing*) Don't play these games with me . . .

Laurence Is that all you can think of to say?

Michel Don't you trust me?

Laurence Don't try and twist the situation.

Michel I'm asking you. Don't you trust me?

Laurence Should I?

Michel decides to risk everything.

Michel Paul couldn't have called you this afternoon, because he was with me.

Laurence You were with Paul this afternoon? You cancelled your meeting to spend the afternoon with Paul?

Michel Yes.

They look at each other, straight in the eye. A very tense moment. A moment of truth? Suddenly, she bursts out laughing.

You think this is funny? Honestly, you think this is funny?

Laurence Oh, it's all right . . . I just wanted to test your alibi.

Michel You wanted to test my alibi? I tell you what I've done today, I explain to you that my best friend is on the brink of depression, my best friend, you hear what I'm saying? My friend for twenty years! A man who's almost

24

a brother to me and you're setting traps for me? I'm your husband, Laurence, you're my wife . . . How can you do a thing like that?

Laurence Because you started off by telling me you'd been to this meeting . . .

Michel I don't see the connection.

Laurence How can you expect me to trust you, when you were lying to me point-blank?

Michel I was being discreet. Out of respect for Paul . . . I don't see the harm in it. Whereas you, you see harm in everything. And do you know why I don't, why I don't see harm in everything? Do you know why?

Laurence No. . .

Michel Because I love you.

Laurence And I don't love you, is that it?

Michel I didn't say that. All I'm saying is that there's no point in having an argument about nothing.

Laurence (*amused*) You're right. I'm sorry.

Pause.

Michel (*calmer*) It's true . . .

Laurence Yes, you're right . . .

Michel Yes . . .

Pause.

Anyway, what did he say?

Laurence Who?

Michel Well, Paul . . . On the phone . . .

Pause. Michel realises he's confused the various versions.

You know, I still can't get over the way the bastards threw him out. Don't you think?

Laurence Yes, you keep saying that.

Michel That's because I still can't get over it. You know, those people have no decency, really. No, it's true: they take you, they use you up and throw you away . . .

Laurence Great. You going to open that bottle?

He's been holding it in his hand for some time.

Michel What? Yes, I'll open it.

Pause.

Laurence Michel . . . can I ask you a question?

Michel Yes, my love.

Laurence Do you still love me?

Michel What a question! Of course I love you.

Laurence No, listen, tell me the truth . . .

Michel (*very sincere*) I love you very very much.

Laurence Then why have we stopped making love?

Michel (*caught off-guard*) What?

Laurence Why have we stopped making love?

The cork comes out of the bottle.

Michel What are you talking about?

Laurence I'm just asking a question, that's all.

Michel But we haven't stopped making love . . . My love. Have we?

Laurence We have.

Michel (*as if he'd never realised*) Oh, have we?

Laurence Well, almost.

Michel (*trying to put things in perspective*) Almost, almost . . . You're exaggerating. I mean, it's true that at the moment . . . I'm knackered. I'm too busy, you know that . . . There seems no end to it.

Laurence All those meetings. . .

Michel Yes. Can't wait for the holidays.

He pours two glasses of wine.

There you are.

Laurence Thanks.

Michel Why did you ask me that?

Laurence No reason.

Michel Do you think I don't love you?

Laurence Sometimes, yes . . .

Michel Please . . . Think whatever you like. But don't think I don't love you. Ever.

Laurence smiles at him.

You promise?

Laurence Yes.

Michel To you, my love.

Laurence (*melancholy*) To us . . .

Blackout.

THREE
THE LIE

A hotel room very similar to the one in the first scene.
Michel and Alice.

Alice So then? What did you say to her?

Michel My wife? I told her I had a meeting in Bordeaux.

Alice In Bordeaux?

Michel Yes. With some clients.

Alice And she believed you?

Michel Why wouldn't she believe me?

Alice Because it sounds really fishy.

Michel What do you mean, 'fishy'? It doesn't sound at all fishy.

Alice It does a bit . . .

Michel Not at all.

Alice I think it does . . . I mean, it smells so much like a lie.

Michel I could easily be in Bordeaux with some clients. I don't see what makes that . . . It doesn't sound fishy at all! Why do you say it sounds fishy?

Alice If my husband told me that, well, honestly . . .

Michel Obviously! Your husband's unemployed! How could he go to Bordeaux to meet some clients?

Alice Why are you getting annoyed?

Michel I'm not getting annoyed. You're the one who said my excuse is fishy. When I could easily be in Bordeaux.

Short pause.

With some clients.

Pause.

What did you tell Paul?

Alice I'm with my aunt.

Michel You're with your aunt?

Alice Yes.

Michel Does your aunt live in Bordeaux?

Alice No. She lives in Chartres.

Michel Then you're supposed to be in Chartres?

Alice That's right.

Michel I imagine you're spending the night in her house.

Alice Yes.

Michel Chartres is an hour from Paris. Aren't you tempted to go back after dinner?

Alice No. You see, she's about to move house.

Michel Your aunt?

Alice Yes. She wanted me to help her sort out a few things. Things which belonged to my mother. Back when . . . you know, back when they were little. She was wondering if some of these things might interest me . . . That's why we planned to spend the evening together. We'll probably finish quite late . . .

Short pause.

Michel (*admiringly*) Very sophisticated.

Alice It's not sophisticated. It's just not fishy.

Michel But why do you say it sounds fishy? I admit my excuse is probably not as sophisticated as yours, but it's no less believable . . .

Alice You reckon?

Michel (*trying to convince himself*) Yes. I could easily be in Bordeaux. With some clients.

Alice (*amused*) In any case, whether we're in Bordeaux or Chartres, I'm very happy to have a night all to ourselves.

Michel Me too. You were right. We needed to go somewhere together.

They approach one another.

Alice Yes. But don't you think it's a bit like being back in our room?

Michel Our room in Paris? You think so?

Alice A bit. Don't you think?

Michel Not really.

Alice I'd say it was identical . . .

Michel It's true there's a bed. But apart from that . . .

Alice (*kissing him*) A bed? Where?

Alice's mobile rings. She looks embarrassed.

Michel Take it, if you like.

Alice It's Paul.

Michel Ah.

Alice I won't take it.

Michel Just as you like.

Alice No.

Pause.

He's not leaving a message . . .

Michel Next thing he'll be calling your aunt on her landline.

Alice You think so?

Michel Possible.

Alice Shit. I ought to have taken it. Why didn't I take it? I'll call him back. It won't upset you, will it? Only be a minute. Why did he call me? This hour of night . . . I hope he's not calling my aunt . . .

Short pause.

Line's busy. Shit.

Michel He doesn't have your aunt's number, though, does he . . .? Does he?

She doesn't answer.

Oh, he does have your aunt's number.

Alice It's in the notebook next to the phone . . .

Michel laughs.

Why are you laughing? I just told you his line's busy? If it turns out . . . Why are you laughing?

Michel Because, I don't want to piss you off, but your story about going to have dinner with your aunt, it's really fishy.

Michel's mobile rings. He glances casually at the number on his screen. He suddenly stops laughing.

Shush. It's my wife. Shit. I'd better take it. Shush . . . Hello? Yes. How are you, darling? Yes. Fine. And you? I know. I know. What? Well, you know, it's going fine.

Anyway, it's going all right. Bordeaux is a magnificent city. Magnificent! The river, all that . . . What? I know.

Alice's mobile starts ringing again. She signals to warn him she wants to take the call.

Just a minute, darling, I need to hang up . . . Yes. My client. I'll be with you in a minute, I'm just speaking to my wife. Whom I love. There's a client on the other line, darling. One of the Bordeaux clients. Yes. Me too. Love you.

He hangs up. She answers.

Alice Hello? I just missed your call. Yes. Yes. Yes. What? She's very well. The move is going well. Mm? You want a word with her?

Michel signals no.

She's a bit tired . . . Is there something you'd like me to say to her? What? You want to speak to her? It's her birthday? Is it? No, I didn't realise . . .

She looks at Michel, who shakes his head.

She doesn't want to speak to you. I've no idea. Why?

Michel indicates he has no idea either.

She has no idea. What? What are you saying? . . . Darling. Paul . . . Of course I'm in Chartres. You don't believe me? What's the matter with you? I could easily put her on. Yes, I could. Why don't I? What? Because I'm hurt. That's right. By your attitude. How can you say that? . . . How can you be so suspicious? . . . Don't you trust me? Paul . . . You don't believe me? All right, here she is.

She holds the mobile out to Michel. He's paralysed.

It's Paul . . . he wants to wish you happy birthday.

A pause which seems interminable. Finally Michel assumes the voice of an old woman.

Michel Hello? Yes. It's Auntie . . .

Alice signals to him to put his hand over the speaker.

Alice She's not a hundred . . .

He goes back on with a different voice.

Michel Oh, thank you! Everything's fine. We're moving, you know, moving . . . Yes . . . Yes . . . Yes . . . Yes, yes. Yes, yes. Yes, yes, yes. Who? Pierrot?

He puts his hand over the speaker.

Who's Pierrot?

Alice Your husband.

Michel (*back to the old woman voice*) Yes, no, he's stepped out . . .

Alice signals . . . He puts his hand over the speaker.

Alice He's dead.

Michel Oh, shit.

Pause.

(*Old woman's voice.*) He stepped out of our lives far too early . . . Yes. Yes. Where? Montauban? Er, um . . . With Frédéric? Um, er . . . In August? Yes. Won't be a minute.

Hand over the speaker.

It's getting complicated.

Alice My aunt's brother, Frédéric, my uncle, has invited us to spend a week in August in his house in Montauban.

Michel (*struggling to memorise this*) Your aunt's brother, Frédéric, your uncle in other words, has invited me . . . Where is Montauban?

Alice What's it matter?

Michel Right, you're right. What should I say?

33

Alice I don't know . . .

Michel I'll just improvise . . .

Alice No!

Michel (*old woman's voice*) So, Montauban, that's all fine. Yes. Don't forget your swimming costume! What? I know it's not on the sea. Yes, Frédéric's had a swimming pool built. I know. Oh . . . I couldn't agree more! Hefty investment, a swimming pool . . . I know. Oh, that's exactly what I said to him! But you know what he's like, your brother, what's that, yes, I mean, my brother, Frédéric, I mean, he never listens to a word I say. Yes. Erm . . . er . . . oh? Erm . . . really? Erm . . . No, well as you know, I'm allergic to pistachios.

Alice, worried by the turn the conversation is taking, reaches for the phone.

Alice Hello? Yes, it's me. Listen, we've got lots more to do . . . we're going to say goodbye.

She glances at Michel, who looks extremely proud of his impersonation.

I know. No, she's not at her best. No, you're exaggerating . . .

She laughs.

No, that's over the top . . . No, you are wicked . . . Stop it . . .

Michel watches her laughing with her husband. He doesn't look best pleased.

Michel (*his normal voice*) What is it?

Alice No, you're exaggerating . . .

Alice laughs some more. She moves away a bit.

Michel (*annoyed*) I really don't see what's so funny . . .

Alice I'll look after it. Sure. Me too. Love you. Yes . . . yes . . . See you tomorrow.

She hangs up.

Michel Well?

Alice What?

Michel All right?

Alice Yes.

Michel What about the aunt thing? See, it worked . . .

Alice I don't know.

Michel Yes, it worked. Like a knife through butter.

Alice What was that thing about pistachios?

Michel What?

Alice That thing about pistachios . . .

Michel A false trail.

Alice A false trail?

Michel (*rather proud of himself*) Yes. Paul knows I absolutely love pistachios. That's why. It occurred to me to say your aunt was allergic to them. See?

Alice Not really, no.

Michel Simple. Since he knows I'm crazy about pistachios, he . . .

Alice (*not listening*) Sometimes I think he could find out any minute . . .

Michel No, no.

Alice (*elsewhere*) Yes. Any minute . . .

Pause.

Michel Right.

Alice What?

Michel Where were we?

He moves over and tries to kiss her again. She pulls away.

What's the matter?

Alice Nothing, it's just . . . That phone call . . .

Michel Life is full of interruptions, but . . .

Alice I'm sorry.

Michel What?

Alice I know it was me who asked you to . . . to come away with me somewhere . . . But I'm not sure it was such a good idea . . . Breaks my heart to think of him all on his own in Paris.

Michel He's not doing anything this evening?

Alice No.

Michel Staying in?

Alice Yes.

Michel Poor old sod . . .

Short pause.

You want to call him back?

Alice It's not that.

Michel What is it, then?

Alice I'm feeling guilty.

Michel Alice . . .

Alice I know. But just having talked to him on the phone . . .

Michel Kiss me.

Alice I feel too guilty. It's true. I think of Paul and I feel like I'm living a permanent lie.

Michel A lie?

Alice Yes. Permanently.

Michel Where is this lie?

Alice Everywhere.

Michel You're not lying to him, Alice. You're just not telling him the truth. It's not the same thing at all!

Alice Of course I'm lying to him. And you are too, you're lying to him.

Michel (*shocked that anyone could think such a thing*) Me? I'm lying to him?

Alice Yes. You're not telling your best friend the truth.

Michel (*trying to get out of it with a glib phrase*) What is the truth, Alice? Mm? What is it? Even philosophers aren't capable of answering that question. So your husband . . .

Alice Sometimes I tell myself I ought to tell him everything.

Michel What?

Alice I tell myself I ought to tell him everything.

Michel Paul?

Alice Yes. Don't you think we ought to?

Michel What do you mean, *we* ought to?

Alice You and me. Tell him the truth. About us. After all, he's your best friend . . .

Michel (*terrified by this idea*) Exactly! Are you crazy? You mustn't tell him anything, Alice. You absolutely mustn't tell him anything. That would be really . . . Can you imagine? Finding out your wife is sleeping with one of your best friends . . . How disgusting it would be. Deeply disgusting. It would destroy him.

Alice Lying to him is destroying me.

Michel Lying to him is destroying you?

Alice Yes.

Michel You've never had a problem with it before . . .

Alice It's true. But now it's, you know, eating me up from inside. I've just realised it. I've had enough of living a lie. Of living like this . . . And I'm wondering if I don't just need to tell him the truth.

Michel You *need* to tell Paul the truth?

Alice I think so, yes.

Michel What about him, does he *need* your truth? Think about it. What's he going to be able to do with it? You'll just be hurting him for no reason.

Alice At least I'd be being honest.

Michel 'At least I'd be being honest . . .' Alice, you're not serious . . .

Alice I am.

Michel Don't be ridiculous. You think you'll feel better once you've told him that for some time you've been sleeping with someone else? Mm? And that, as it happens, that someone else is *me*?

Alice Yes, I think I will feel better.

Michel Very selfish.

Alice Perhaps.

Michel What is the problem, Alice? All right, fine, you're cheating on your husband. And you're lying to him. But, Alice, you're doing it *for his sake*. I mean, the fact you're not telling him the truth.

Alice For his sake?

Michel Yes. Out of respect for him. To protect him. To spare him. Not to hurt him. It would be selfish to tell him the truth just to relieve your conscience. Yes. Very selfish. You have no right to do that, Alice. You have no right. You'll destroy everything.

Pause.

And anyway, to be honest, I don't see what business it is of his . . .

Alice You don't see what business it is of his?

Michel No.

Alice That his best friend has been sleeping with his wife for the best part of a year . . .

Michel (*trying to put things in perspective*) For a few months, Alice, a few months. Let's not exaggerate.

Alice That they meet in hotel rooms. And you don't see what business it is of his . . .

Michel All right, if you like, maybe it is his business, but only *indirectly*.

Alice Indirectly?

Michel Yes. Through intermediaries.

Alice I'm being serious, Michel.

Michel Me too, Alice.

39

Alice What about you, have you never wanted to come clean?

Michel To Paul?

Alice To your wife.

Michel No.

Alice You aren't worn out with lying to her?

Michel It's the price I have to pay to see you.

Alice You're going to say I'm naive, but sometimes I think everything would be so much simpler if everyone told the truth . . .

Michel It'd be a nightmare, Alice. It'd be a total nightmare. If people, from one day to the next, stopped lying to one another, there wouldn't be one couple left on Earth. It would be more or less the end of civilisation.

Alice You don't understand. I live with him. And I love him.

Michel Paul?

Alice Yes.

Michel Obviously you love him. Obviously. And I love him too. I love him very much. Let me remind you, he's my best friend . . . But the only way we can demonstrate our love for him, given the current state of affairs, is to lie to him.

Alice Maybe.

Michel Of course . . . Especially now, Alice. Especially right now. Let me remind you, he's unemployed . . . It's no joke living with that. Believe me. The last thing he needs is details of your sex life. Mm?

Alice Maybe.

Michel Of course . . .

Alice When are you seeing him?

Michel Monday. We're playing tennis . . . Why?

Alice No reason.

Michel But, Alice . . . promise me you won't say anything to him.

Short pause.

It's really important. You mustn't tell him . . . Will you promise me not to say anything to him?

Short pause.

Mm, Alice, will you promise me?

Alice No.

Blackout.

FOUR
FRIENDSHIP

Michel and Paul, who've been playing tennis. They have all their gear (rackets, etc.) with them.

Michel Anyway, how are you?

Paul That's the tenth time you've asked me, Michel.

Michel Is it? I'm sorry. But, you know, at my age . . .

Paul You repeat yourself. Yes, you already said that. What's the matter with you today?

Michel What? Nothing. I'm losing my memory.

Paul Since when?

Michel (*attempting a feeble joke*) I can't remember.

He laughs on his own. Pause. He's obviously uncomfortable.

Good match, at least.

Paul Think so? I didn't play well.

Michel Didn't play well? You won.

Paul Yes. But only because you didn't play well either. I mean, I never thought you were a great tennis player. But I could always tell the difference between you and, let's say for example, a beginner. Not today, though.

Michel What do you expect, I'm getting old . . . By the way, you never told me how it went, your interview . . . For that job . . .

Paul I don't know.

Michel I thought it went well.

Paul Who told you that?

Michel What? Nobody. Why, did it go badly?

Paul No, no. It went well. I mean, you know, it's always difficult to tell.

Michel Of course. Even so, you felt it went well?

Paul Fairly well, yes . . .

Michel Always trust your instincts.

Paul Funny you should say that.

Michel Say what?

Paul That you should always trust your instincts.

Michel Why?

Paul Because I had a strange instinct today, just now.

Michel Oh? What was that?

42

Paul I had an instinct you were letting me win.

Michel The tennis match?

Paul Yes.

Michel What?

Paul What I said.

Michel Why would I let you win?

Paul I don't know. Just an instinct.

Michel You know very well I can't stand losing . . .

Paul Yes, I know that.

Michel Then why would I let you win?

Paul Precisely, that's what I was wondering.

Michel No. You won, that's all.

Paul You weren't on form.

Michel It's those balls . . . Where d'you buy them?

Paul The balls?

Michel Yes.

Paul Can't remember. I mean, they're the same balls as last week.

Michel Are they?

Paul Yes.

Pause.

Yes. They said they'd call me back in a few days.

Michel The Swedes? Fingers crossed, then . . .

Paul How are you?

Michel All right. Lots of work . . .

43

He realises he's been rather tactless.

Sorry. . .

Paul Why don't you take a few days off? You don't look
great . . .

Michel Me? You're only saying that because you beat me
for once.

Paul I mean it . . . You're working too hard. You ought
to take a weekend off . . . Get some fresh ideas . . . Go
away somewhere . . .

Michel Mm? Maybe.

Paul Didn't you just have a weekend away?

Michel Me?

Paul Yes. The other day . . .

Michel Mm? Yes. But it was for work.

Paul That's what I'm saying . . . you're working too hard.

Michel (*trying a joke to change the subject*) More than
we can say for you . . .

He realises it isn't funny.

Sorry.

Paul's mobile rings.

Paul Oh . . . Excuse me, it's Alice . . . Just a minute . . .
Hello? Yes, darling. No, I'm still with Michel. Yes. We've
finished. No, I won . . .

Michel It was close.

Paul What? Sure . . . Fine. Thanks. Me too. Love you
too. See you soon.

He hangs up.

She was calling from her office.

Michel Oh, yes?

Paul Yes.

Pause.

Michel (*innocently*) Is she all right?

Paul I think so. How do you think she is at the moment?

Michel What?

Paul How do you think she is?

Michel Alice?

Paul Yes.

Michel (*scenting danger*) You mean . . .

Paul My wife.

Michel No, I mean . . . in what way?

Paul You haven't noticed anything special?

Michel No. Why?

Paul I don't know. She's different.

Michel Alice?

Paul Yes.

Michel I don't think so. Quite the opposite. I don't think she's changed at all. On the other hand, I haven't seen much of her lately . . . What makes you say that?

Paul I don't know.

Pause.

And how's Laurence? Everything all right between you?

Michel What? Yes, fine.

Paul You know I spoke to her on the phone the other day . . .

Michel Alice?

Paul No, Laurence.

Michel How come?

Paul I was trying to find you. But your mobile was switched off. And you weren't at your office.

Michel Oh, yes? When?

Paul I don't know. The other day . . .

Michel You called the landline?

Paul Yes.

Michel And you spoke to Laurence?

Paul Yes. She wasn't teaching. Because of the strike.

Michel Oh, yes?

Paul She seemed all right, is she?

Michel (*elsewhere*) Yes.

   Pause.

Paul I had lunch with Antoine Libéri yesterday. You know who I mean?

Michel (*still elsewhere*) No.

Paul A guy I was at university with. I've mentioned him to you several times. We hadn't seen each other for years . . .

Michel Oh, yes? Great . . . But listen . . . Did you just say you'd spoken to Laurence on the phone?

Paul (*amused*) Yes.

Michel (*visibly rattled*) Oh.

Paul Why?

Michel You never usually ring the landline.

Paul I couldn't find you.

Michel Was it that urgent?

Paul Yes and no. I wanted to talk to you about Alice. As it happens . . .

Short pause.

You know, she's an extraordinary woman.

Michel I know.

Paul You do?

Michel Yes.

Short pause.

I mean, I imagine she is . . . Why did you say she was different?

Paul She's an extraordinary woman. Especially when you're going through a sticky patch. This'll probably seem strange to you, but since I've been out of work, she's been wonderful to me. So kind. It's times like this you remember what a family is all about. She's incredibly touching.

Michel Is that what you wanted to say to me on the landline?

Paul No. I wanted to . . . How can I put this? She's so exceptionally thoughtful, I . . . I mean, I'm not sure how to explain it to you. I think she's feeling guilty. She's not comfortable about something. She's overcompensating.

Michel You think so?

Paul Frankly, I think she's having an affair.

Michel Alice?

Paul Yes.

Michel Alice, having an affair?

Paul Yes.

Michel No, Paul . . . *Alice?*

Paul In fact, I'm convinced of it.

Michel Paul, you're imagining things. I mean, think for a minute: *Alice!*

Paul No, I'm telling you. I know she is. I have absolutely no doubt about it.

Michel *Alice?* But that's . . . terrible.

Paul No. Happens all the time.

Michel You're so calm. It's admirable. If that happened to me, I'd . . . No, I do admire you. For taking things so philosophically. (*Innocently.*) Any idea who the bastard is?

Paul No. Obviously I'm wondering who it might be.

Michel Obviously, yes. That's obvious.

Paul Yes.

Michel Obviously.

Pause.

What a bastard!

Pause.

Paul Yes. I'm pretty sure I had him on the phone the other day . . .

Michel Who, the bastard?

Paul Yes. Alice told me she'd gone to see her aunt. But she hadn't.

Michel What are you talking about? Of course she had . . . Aren't you being a bit paranoid?

Paul No, I'm telling you. I phoned her aunt. Alice wasn't there.

Michel Oh.

Paul So then I called her on her mobile. And she put on this rather grotesque show for me. The man she was with pretended to be her aunt, he was just hopeless . . .

Michel As bad as that?

Paul Yes. I can't tell you, really hopeless. I felt embarrassed for him.

Pause. Michel is very upset on Paul's behalf.

Michel Shit!

Pause.

What are you going to do?

Paul (*looking Michel straight in the eye*) I can't decide if confrontation is the best idea.

Michel (*paling*) You just told me you don't know who he is . . .

Paul No, I wasn't talking about the bastard.

Michel (*relieved*) Oh . . .

Paul I was talking about Alice. I can't decide whether to confront her . . .

Michel Well, if you want my advice, whatever you do, don't confront her.

Paul What?

Michel Don't say a word to her. You don't want to lose her, do you? Then just wait. Be patient. Softly, softly . . .

Her adventure will run out of steam of its own accord and she'll come back to you. She'll come back and you'll completely forget about the whole thing . . . I promise you.

Paul Maybe.

Michel I'm telling you. If you try to talk to her about it, it'll be fatal, it'll end in disaster. You don't want your relationship to end in disaster, do you? So don't say a word to her.

Paul Your advice is to pretend I know nothing about it.

Michel Yes. Just wait. Especially as it's already happened to you.

Paul What has?

Michel You told me it had already happened to you. Having an affair. See. If Alice had found out about it at the time, you'd have split up.

Paul Maybe.

Michel See. No, believe me. Don't say a word to her.

Paul I expect you're right.

Pause.

The other day, as I was saying, I had lunch with this friend of mine, Antoine Libéri, I was really happy to see him again. Because, you know, we'd been very close, he and I, inseparable, and here we were, together again after all those years, and we didn't have a single thing to say to each other.

Michel Oh?

Paul No. It's the most painful thing about getting old, I think: watching your friends change.

Michel What do you mean?

Paul Dying starts happening long before actual physical death. That's what I said to myself when I came out of that lunch. You watch your friends dying long before they *actually* die: you recognise their voices, their faces, their expressions, but inside, they're not the same people any more. So there comes a moment in your life, inevitably, when you're *alone*. Friendless.

Michel Why are you telling me this?

Paul Because you're my friend. My best friend.

Blackout.

FIVE
THE BREAK-UP

Alice's surgery. The middle of the day. Her waiting room is full, but she's making a call on her mobile between appointments.

Alice (*on the phone*) Yes, yes. And it's been troubling you since when? Monday . . . Do you wear glasses? You don't. Then perhaps we'd better give you a check-up. Yes, I expect that's the reason. Could account for the dizziness. That's right. So, wait, let's have a look . . . I can offer you . . .

Michel comes in.

Michel Alice, I have to talk to you.

Alice is surprised to see him barging in. He's clearly not expected. She motions to him to keep quiet. She checks her diary. Michel paces: he looks very agitated.

Alice (*on the phone*) I can offer you . . . How's Wednesday morning? . . . No? All right. Then that leaves us Thursday. No, on Tuesday I'm afraid I . . .

Michel Alice, I . . .

Alice (*on the phone*) Yes, I see. But I can't manage Tuesday. Sorry. On the other hand, if you're free on Thursday . . . Yes? You could do Thursday?

Michel Alice, I . . .

Alice (*on the phone*) I've a slot in the morning. Yes, between ten and eleven. Oh? Yes, no, I can't really say . . . Absolutely. Yes, I do have to run late sometimes. So I couldn't guarantee . . . No, I don't really know.

Michel Alice, this is urgent . . .

Alice (*annoyed with Michel, still on the phone*) I see, I see. No problem. Listen, the simplest thing is for you to call my secretary. Yes. It's the easiest way to make an appointment. Yes. Thank you. Not at all. See you Thursday. Goodbye.

She hangs up.

So now you're barging into my surgery . . .

Michel It's urgent. I know your waiting room is full, I know . . .

Alice And I'm running behind . . .

Michel Yes, yes. But I need to speak with you for two minutes. Two minutes.

Alice What is it?

Michel Have you spoken to Paul?

Alice What?

Michel I'm asking if you've spoken to Paul.

Alice What about?

Michel What do you think about?

Alice Why are you asking me?

Michel I've just been with him. Playing tennis. *He knows.*

Alice What?

Michel *He knows.*

Alice What makes you think that?

Michel I don't know. Insinuations. I know he knows.

Alice Insinuations?

Michel Yes.

Alice What did he insinuate?

Michel Mm? Did you say something to him? Last time we saw each other, you kept saying you wanted to tell him everything.

Alice Michel . . .

Michel What?

Alice I don't like you barging into my surgery like this. If you need to talk to me, leave me a message. We can arrange a meeting. But not like this. Not where I work. I can't have that.

Michel I'm sorry. I just couldn't wait.

Alice Why?

Michel I need to know.

Alice What did he insinuate?

Michel Nothing. He told me you were really there for him, really kind . . .

Alice So?

Michel I can't remember how he put it, but it was as if he was blaming me for something . . .

Alice You?

Michel Yes. That's why. He told me he thought you were having an affair.

Alice He told you that?

Michel Yes. He said it was like you were overcompensating, that you seemed uncomfortable . . . in short, that you were feeling guilty about something.

Alice What else did he say?

Michel Nothing specific . . .

Alice Apparently he won your tennis match . . .

Michel What? What's that got to do with it?

Alice I thought you were better than him.

Michel I am better than him. But that's nothing to do with . . . Alice, did you hear what I said? He knows, Alice, he knows *everything*!

Alice Listen, stretch out there and relax for a minute . . .

Michel I don't want to stretch out there! How am I supposed to relax? He's found out everything.

Alice He hasn't found out anything.

Michel Yes, he has! He's found out everything!

Pause.

(*Solemnly.*) We have to talk, Alice.

Alice What do you think we're doing?

Michel We can't go on seeing each other as things stand. He told me he spoke to my wife on the phone. You understand? He called her on the landline . . . My wife . . . It can't go on like this . . .

Alice No.

Michel You understand what I'm saying?

Alice Yes.

Michel I need you to understand . . .

Alice I just told you, I understand.

Michel It's too dangerous . . . It'd be more sensible to . . . I mean, to leave it . . . To make a joint decision not to . . . No, listen, wait. Let me finish . . . Wait . . .

Alice The waiting room's full, Michel.

Michel Well, they can wait five minutes. Isn't that what it's for, a waiting room?

Alice We'll talk about this later.

Michel I think we're going to have to break up.

Pause.

Aren't you going to say anything?

Alice What do you want me to say?

Michel Tell me the truth.

Alice What truth?

Michel Stop it, Alice. You know very well what I'm talking about.

Alice I don't.

Michel I want to know if you've told him about us . . .

Alice What difference does it make?

Michel What difference does it make? All the difference in the world.

Alice I thought you weren't interested in the truth.

Michel Alice . . . Have you told him? Have you told him you were having an affair?

Short pause.

Alice Yes.

Michel I knew it.

Alice I had no choice.

Michel You promised me you wouldn't tell him.

Alice I couldn't go on lying to him, Michel. It wasn't possible.

Michel You realise what you've done?

Alice When I got back the other day, he looked me in the eye . . . He knew perfectly well I hadn't been with my aunt. He knew it. What could I have done? I couldn't bear the way he was looking at me . . . I started crying. And I told him everything. There we are.

Michel What did you tell him? I mean . . . you didn't tell him it was *me*? Did you?

Alice At the very least I owed him an explanation, don't you think?

Michel Yes, I suppose so, but did you tell him it was *me*?

Alice Of course I did.

Michel You mean he knows? That, just now, when we were playing tennis . . .

Alice Yes.

Michel He behaved as if nothing had . . . And he knew!

Pause. It's dawning on him.

Michel We played tennis, we had a drink, we talked like old friends . . . And he knew? What a bastard!

Alice Michel . . .

Michel And he's supposed to be my best friend . . . It's true, you can't trust anybody. Not even your best friend!

Alice You don't think you've got it the wrong way round . . . ?

Michel And what did he say? About me? What did he say?

Alice Nothing.

Michel What do you mean, nothing?

Alice What I say, nothing.

Michel Tell me the truth, Alice. Enough lies! You told him you'd been sleeping with his best friend for several months and he said nothing?

Alice All he said was he'd known for ages.

Michel What?

Alice He told me he'd known for months. And that he was relieved I'd finally told him the truth.

Michel He'd known for months?

Alice That's what he said.

Michel He'd known what for months? That I'd been sleeping with you? Is that what you're trying to tell me?

Alice Yes. He's known from the beginning.

Michel But that's impossible. I mean, Alice . . .

Alice All the same.

Michel He's known we were sleeping together from the beginning and he never said anything to me about it? He's been pretending for months? You mean for months he's been fucking with me?

Pause, during which Michel takes this in.

What a bastard!

Very short pause.

How could he do that to me? To me! How could he?

Pause.

(*Very upset.*) But how did he know? How did he know?
I mean . . . How did he know?

Alice I don't know.

Michel Of course you know.

Alice I didn't ask him.

Michel You didn't think to ask him how he found out?

Alice No.

Michel Do you think he would have talked to Laurence
about it? When he was on the phone? On the landline?
Do you think he would have talked to her about it?

Alice Why would he have talked to your wife?

Michel I don't know . . . Revenge.

Alice He's not like that.

Michel Anyway, I have to go and see him.

Alice What?

Michel I need an explanation. Where is he? At home?

Alice Mm? Yes.

Michel I have to go and see him.

Alice Now? I don't think that's a good idea . . . Michel . . .

Michel Why not? I can't go on as if nothing's happened.

Alice Yes, you can. That's exactly what you have to do. Things will settle down. Just like that. Quietly.

Michel It's not possible, Alice. Open your eyes! There's no way we can avoid thrashing it out, him and me. Just think about it. He's been lying to me for *six months*! Six months he's been lying to his best friend!

Alice Michel . . .

Michel Why? Why isn't it a good idea?

Alice I can't tell you why. But believe me, Michel, believe me, it's not a good idea.

Pause.

Blackout.

SIX
AN EXPLANATION

The end of the day. Paul's house.

Michel I must have called you sixty times today . . . Couldn't get through.

Paul I went for a walk. And forgot my phone.

Michel Really?

Paul Yes. Down by the Tuileries. Gorgeous light. See, that's exactly the sort of thing I never noticed before.

Michel (*strangulated*) Before what?

Paul Before I lost my job. I was working all the time and in some ways I missed a lot.

Michel Of course. Nose to the grindstone.

Paul What?

Michel No, I'm just saying, you had your nose . . . I mean, yes, right, you missed a lot.

Paul Yes. I can't quite explain why, but since I've been unemployed, I feel better. It's true. Lighter.

Michel Perhaps you've found your vocation . . .

Paul (*smiling*) Who knows? For example, *before*, I'd never go for a walk.

Michel Really?

Paul No. I never took time to do anything. Vast quantities of things I never even saw. See, I was like a blind man. You see?

Michel Yes.

Paul But now, my eyes are open. I can see what's going on around me. People. Trees. Architecture. The . . .

Michel That's what I wanted to talk to you about.

Paul Oh?

Michel Yes. That's why I came by.

   Pause.

I didn't know you went for walks.

Paul Didn't you?

Michel No.

   Pause.

I came by because I wanted to talk to you.

   Pause.

(*Embarrassed.*) You wouldn't have something to drink, would you?

Paul What would you like?

Michel Something strong.

Paul Whisky?

Michel Perfect.

Paul Ice?

Michel Mm? No, no. As it comes.

Paul pours a whisky for him. Pause.

On your walks, do you always head for the Tuileries?

Paul No, it depends. Why?

Michel Nothing. Just making conversation.

Michel indicates that he'd like another whisky.

Don't hold back . . . Thanks.

Pause. He drinks.

It's good whisky . . . What is it?

Paul Just whisky. Nothing special . . .

Michel Really? It's good.

Pause.

Paul So. What's new since this morning?

Michel What?

Paul If you remember, we played tennis this morning.

Michel Yes. I know. Well, yes, something has happened. That's what I wanted to talk to you about.

Pause. His embarrassment is becoming more and more obvious.

How can I put this? I used to be more of a vodka man . . . Having said I was more of a vodka man, I don't mean that's all I drank. But I never got into the habit of drinking whisky as an aperitif, say . . .

Paul No?

Michel No. I don't know why. My father used to take a small whisky every day. It was almost the first thing he did when he got home. Except he liked ice with it . . .

Paul Your father?

Michel Yes. He liked whisky on the rocks.

Paul Is that what you wanted to talk to me about?

Michel No.

Paul I didn't think so.

Pause.

Michel Well. I went to see Alice just now. In her surgery.

Paul Oh?

Michel Yes.

Very short pause.

What about you, do you ever hear from your father?

Paul Mm? Not since he died.

Michel Oh, yes. Right. Sorry . . . Poor old chap . . .

Pause. Finally, Michel takes the plunge.

So, yes. I went to see her in her surgery. Alice. We talked. And she told me you'd talked as well. And I said to myself it was time you and I talked as well. That we should talk about what you'd talked about.

Paul You're not making yourself entirely clear.

Michel Well, it's about . . . the fact is, that for some time . . . I . . . The point is. She told me you knew.

Paul That I knew what?

Michel About Alice and me, Paul.

Pause. No reaction. Michel is seized by a doubt.

You did know? Mm? Paul . . .

Paul What do you mean by 'Alice and me'?

Michel What?

Paul What are you talking about?

Michel Nothing.

Pause. The doubt increases.

Alice told me you knew.

Paul Knew what?

Michel What?

Pause.

You didn't know?

Pause.

You didn't know.

Paul I did.

Michel You did know?

Paul Yes. From the beginning.

Michel (*relieved*) Ah . . . I thought I'd put my foot in it . . .

Paul I've known from the beginning.

Michel That's what she told me. She told me you'd known all about it from the beginning.

Paul Yes.

Michel I don't understand why you didn't say anything to me about it!

Paul What would you like me to have said?

Michel But I mean, shit, I'm your friend! If you can't confide in your friend, then . . . Why didn't you talk to me?

Paul More for you to talk to me. Don't you think?

Pause.

Michel Listen . . . I'm sorry. I'm so sorry . . . But you must know I'm enormously fond of you . . . I don't know what came over me . . . How these things happen . . . The whole business suddenly seems completely ridiculous . . . And I feel terribly guilty.

Pause.

Paul Another drink?

Michel Please. Thank you. You have one too.

Paul Thanks.

Pause. He swallows some whisky.

Michel You know, I told Alice not to tell you, but she wouldn't listen. She thinks you're always right to tell the truth. I did everything I could, really, everything, to persuade her to go on lying to you. You have to believe me.

Paul I do believe you.

Michel Yes, I did everything I could.

Paul But in some ways it's better like this. Don't you think?

Michel Mm? I don't know.

Pause.

So. I wanted to tell you we're going to stop seeing each other. I mean, Alice and me. I hope we can manage to

stay friends in spite of all this. You and me, I mean . . .
I really hope we can. If you didn't want to see me again,
I'd completely understand, but it would upset me terribly.
There we are, that's what I wanted to tell you.

Pause.

Paul Is that it?

Michel No.

Pause.

So . . . Alice told me you'd known for a long time . . .
That's what you told her. Or at least she, she told me
that's what you told her.

Paul Told her what?

Michel That you'd been aware of this right from the
beginning.

Paul Yes.

Michel How did you find out?

Paul What?

Michel How did you find out I was . . . with your wife.

Paul It's . . .

Michel Yes?

Paul What's it matter?

Michel I'd like to know.

Paul You really want to know?

Michel Yes.

Paul No . . . It's pointless.

Michel Tell me . . . How did you find out?

Paul From your wife.

Michel Excuse me?

Paul Your wife told me.

Pause.

Michel My wife told you what?

Paul That you were sleeping with my wife.

Michel (*not taking him seriously*) Are you joking?

Paul No.

Michel (*devastated*) You mean she knows about it?

Paul Yes.

Michel (*whispering, for fear of being overheard*) She knows about it?

Paul Yes. Has done from the beginning.

Pause. Michel takes this in.

Michel You mean her as well, you mean she's been playacting for six months?

Pause.

Her as well? She's known about it from the beginning and she didn't say anything to me? She watched me going through it, lying to her, trying to be discreet . . . And she knew?

Short pause.

What a bitch!

Paul What?

Michel God, what a bitch! Do you realise how manipulative this woman is? Why didn't she say anything to me? Why?

Paul Ask her . . .

Michel Do you realise? Twenty years of marriage and that's where you get to . . . The discovery that your wife is lying to you, manipulating you, taking you for a . . . What a disaster! God, what a disaster!

Paul She may have had some good reason not to tell you . . .

Michel And you, why didn't you tell me? You arsehole!

Paul I didn't think I had the right.

Michel You didn't think you had the right?

Paul No.

Michel And if I smashed your fucking teeth in, would that give you the right?

Paul Why are you getting upset?

Michel For fuck's sake, I was sleeping with your wife!

Paul I know.

Michel And you're telling me you didn't think you had the right . . .

Paul I thought you were doing it to get back at me.

Michel Mm?

Paul What?

Michel What do you mean, to get back at you? To get back at you for what?

Paul Mm?

Michel I don't understand what you're telling me.

Paul I thought you'd guessed.

Michel Guessed what?

Paul Nothing.

Michel Go on. Tell me . . . Paul . . . Guessed what?

Paul About Laurence and me.

Michel Excuse me?

Paul pours himself another drink.

You've had an affair with Laurence? Paul. You've had an affair with my wife?

Paul Yes . . .

Michel What? Since when?

Paul What's it matter?

Michel Since when?

Paul Since August.

Michel (*devastated*) August last year?

Paul Yes. Or in fact, the year before last.

Pause. Michel takes this in.

Michel Are you telling me you've slept with my wife?

Paul Yes.

Michel (*scandalised*) With my wife? With your best friend's wife?

Paul Yes.

Michel You shit! How can you look at yourself in the mirror? With your best friend's wife! Your best friend, Paul . . . You make me want to throw up.

Paul Didn't stop you sleeping with my wife, if you remember.

Michel Don't try twisting things around! Not with me!

Paul Why are you getting annoyed?

Michel Why am I getting annoyed? You're asking me why I'm getting annoyed? It's true, let's see, why am I getting annoyed? For months my best friend has been sleeping with my wife behind my back, what's to get annoyed about? . . . You want to know why I'm annoyed? Because your attitude disgusts me.

Paul I see.

Michel Well, I don't see. I don't see how my wife could have slept with someone like you. On top of everything else, you haven't even got a job.

Paul At the time, I was finance director . . .

Michel Don't make things worse, please. Don't make things worse . . .

Pause.

And did you tell Alice? Did you tell her you were sleeping with my wife?

Paul Obviously.

Michel (*parodying him*) Obviously.

Paul When I found out you were sleeping with mine, we had a long discussion. And told each other the truth.

Michel When was that?

Paul I don't know. Six months ago. Something like that.

Michel What? You mean she knows?

Paul Yes.

Michel She knew as well, she knew you were sleeping with my wife?

Paul Yes.

Michel Let me get this right, I was the only one who didn't know what was going on, is that it?

Paul You could put it like that.

Michel Marvellous! And did you sometimes have little dinners *à trois*, to discuss the situation?

69

Paul Michel . . .

Michel What? What? You're sleeping with my *wife*, you're sleeping with my *mistress* and you claim to be my best friend . . . You want my job as well, while you're at it?

Paul Calm down.

Michel You want me to calm down?

Paul Yes. Have another drink . . .

Michel Try pouring me one, I warn you, I'm likely to throw it in your face.

Paul Michel . . .

Michel Fuck . . .

Paul Michel . . .

He pours Michel another drink. Pause.

Michel (*calmer*) Alice. Why didn't she say anything to me?

Paul I persuaded her not to.

Michel You?

Paul Yes. She couldn't stand living a lie. She wanted to tell you everything . . . But you kept saying it was no good telling the truth . . .

Michel In other words, the three of you made a total idiot out of me.

Paul On the contrary, Michel. On the contrary. We didn't tell you because we love you.

Michel Yes, yes, don't trouble yourself, I know the routine.

Pause.

And to think that just this morning, so as not to undermine your morale, I deliberately lost our tennis match . . . Makes me sick.

Paul I've been deliberately losing for a year and a half.

Michel What? What did you say?

Paul Nothing.

Michel Yes. What did you say?

Paul I said I've been deliberately losing for a year and a half . . .

Michel Are you serious? Paul, are you serious? What are you implying? That you're a better tennis player than I am? Is that what you're implying?

No answer.

I don't think we have anything more to say to one another.

He gets ready to leave. Pause.

Are you still seeing her?

Paul What?

Michel My wife, I think we were discussing, were we not? I just wanted to find out what kind of play we're in . . . To find out if it's a comedy or a tragedy.

Paul (*a tentative stab at humour*) You never know with a woman . . .

Michel Are you still seeing her?

Paul (*his turn to be embarrassed*) Listen, I think there's something I ought to tell you . . .

Pause.

Blackout.

SEVEN
THE TRUTH

Michel arrives back home. Laurence isn't there.

Michel Laurence! Laurence! Where are you? Anyone about?

He paces up and down the stage.

Where the hell is she? Laurence!

She makes a sudden appearance.

Laurence Why are you shouting like that?

Michel Why am I shouting? You're asking me why I'm shouting?

Laurence Yes.

Michel I'm not shouting, Laurence, I was calling you.

Laurence I was in the dressing room. I didn't hear you.

Michel And may I ask what you were doing in the dressing room?

Laurence (*amused*) Getting ready. What's the matter with you?

Michel Are you going out?

Laurence Yes.

Michel Who with?

Laurence You really want to know?

Michel (*thinking of Paul*) I already know.

Laurence Then why ask?

Michel Just to hear you say it.

Laurence I'm going out with you.

Michel With me?

Laurence Yes.

Michel First I've heard of it.

Laurence We're having dinner with the Bessons this evening. Had you forgotten?

Michel This evening? Are you sure?

Laurence Yes. We need to leave in half an hour . . .

Michel I don't want to go. I want to stay in. I need to talk to you.

Laurence Michel, you can't just cancel at the last minute . . . .

Michel Of course you can. If it's something important . . .

Laurence What's so important?

Pause.

Michel I found something out today. Something important.

Laurence What about?

Michel Paul.

Pause.

I've just come from his place. Just now.

Laurence Oh?

Michel Yes.

Pause.

You know what he claims?

Laurence No.

Michel This'll give you a laugh.

Laurence Tell me.

Michel He claims he's been deliberately letting me win for a year and a half. At tennis . . .

Laurence Paul?

Michel Yes. Since August to be precise. Not last August. No. The August before last.

Laurence He's just saying that because he's no good at it.

Michel I know that . . .

Laurence Then?

Michel See, he thinks he's a terrific tennis player. Whereas his backhand, for example, leaves a great deal to be desired. I say that quite objectively, Laurence. Quite objectively. Paul is a mediocre tennis player.

Laurence I'm not sure what you're getting at.

Michel All right, I'm coming to it.

   Pause.

I went to see him just now and we had a few drinks.

Laurence (*amused*) Yes, I was wondering . . .

Michel There I was, we were chatting, and suddenly he comes out with this.

Laurence With what?

Michel He announces that all this time he's been letting me win. Seriously questioning all my victories. All of them, without exception. Can you believe that?

Laurence What's it matter?

Michel You're asking me . . .

74

Laurence You're not playing to win. Are you?

Michel How could I trust a friend who admits he's been lying to me all this time?

Pause.

I know everything, Laurence.

Laurence You know everything?

Michel Yes.

Laurence What about?

Michel What do you think?

Laurence indicates she has no idea.

See, you're going on with it.

Laurence Going on with what?

Michel The playacting. The lies . . .

Laurence Me?

Michel I said, I know everything. I've just come from Paul's. He told me everything!

Laurence What are you talking about, Michel?

Michel I trusted you, Laurence.

Laurence Do you mind being a bit clearer?

Michel But I'm telling you, I know, I know everything and you persist with this miserable little part you've been playing for a year and a half. A year and a half! Eighteen months!

Laurence You've had too much to drink, Michel.

Michel That has nothing to do with it.

Laurence Then why are you attacking me like this? For no reason . . .

Michel For no reason? For no reason, Laurence? When you've been cheating on me for a year and a half?

Laurence Me?

Michel Yes, you.

Laurence Absolutely not.

Michel See, you just go on denying it.

Laurence Damn right I'm denying it.

Michel Am I dreaming? . . .

Laurence So wake up. What is all this?

Michel I told you, he told me everything.

Laurence Who? Paul? Paul told you I was cheating on you?

Michel Yes. And guess who with?

Laurence No idea. But I'd be fascinated to know . . .

Michel With my best friend.

Laurence With Paul?

Michel Precisely.

Laurence starts laughing.

Yes, me too, I had a good laugh as well to start off with . . .

Laurence This is just stupid, Michel.

Michel I totally agree with you. It's stupid. Stupid and cruel. How could you do that to me? My best friend . . .

Laurence (*almost wanting to laugh*) Paul told you that? He told you I'd been sleeping with him for a year?

Michel A year and a half.

Laurence Whatever.

76

Michel And it's still going on . . .

Laurence (*laughing*) It's not true, I can assure you!
Listen, darling, it doesn't make sense for a minute. What
would I be doing with Paul? I've always thought he was
very nice . . . But seriously . . . If I'm married to you, I'm
not going to take Paul for a lover . . .

Michel What do you mean?

Laurence Obvious, isn't it? You're better-looking than
him. You're more intelligent than him. You have a better
sense of humour . . .

Michel I'm better at tennis.

Laurence Yes. And on top of all that, I love you. I really
think you've had too much to drink, if you're believing
that sort of thing.

Pause.

Michel You make me sick with your lies, all of you! Am
I the only honest one? Am I the only one who doesn't
spend all his time lying? You're lying to me. Paul's lying
to me! Alice is lying.

Laurence What's Alice got to do with it?

Michel Listen . . . I've just come from Paul's. We said
everything there was to say. Everything, you understand
me? There are no more secrets between us. We talked
about my relationship with Alice, as well as yours . . . So
please, just stop lying to me. . .

Laurence (*her mood abruptly changing*) Your relationship
with Alice?

Michel Well, I mean . . . 'relationship' . . . It's a big word.

Laurence What relationship?

Michel Mm?

Laurence Are you telling me you've had an affair with Alice?

Michel Don't pretend you didn't know.

Laurence You've had an affair with Alice . . .

Michel You know all about it. You're the one who told Paul about it.

Laurence And how long has this relationship been going on?

Michel Hardly any time. Six months.

Laurence Six months?

Michel Hardly.

Laurence You call that hardly any time?

Michel Yes, compared to yours. It's one-third of a year and a half.

Laurence Why are you telling me this? Out of the blue . . . So crudely . . .

Michel I've told you, because you already know about it!

Laurence I know about it?

Michel Of course you do . . .

Laurence About your relationship with Alice? I know about it?

Michel Yes. From the beginning.

Laurence Oh, yes?

Michel Yes. And you carried on as if nothing was happening. For months . . .

Laurence Paul tell you that as well?

Michel Yes. From the beginning you've carried on as if nothing was happening. That's what's killing me . . .

Imagining you pretending all that time . . . How can you expect me to trust you from now on?

Pause. She's shattered.

Laurence You realise what you're doing?

Michel I'm talking to you sincerely. I'm asking you to stop lying to me.

Laurence You don't understand a thing.

Michel *I* don't understand a thing?

Laurence Not a thing.

Michel What don't I understand?

Laurence Never mind.

Michel No. Go on. Tell me.

Laurence I've never had an affair with Paul. Never. If he told you that, it was only to . . .

Michel To what?

Laurence I don't know . . . Because he thought you might be stupid enough to come and admit to me off your own bat that you'd had an affair with Alice.

Michel What?

Laurence It's revenge . . .

Michel You really think Paul is that twisted?

Laurence Yes.

Michel (*defending Paul*) May I remind you, you're speaking of my best friend!

Laurence You really are too idiotic, Michel.

Michel What?

Laurence Can you really imagine me with Paul?

Michel I'm not that depraved.

Laurence It's grotesque. I've never had an affair with Paul. Never.

Pause. Michel is starting to have doubts.

Michel I'm not sure I believe you . . .

Laurence It's the truth. Sorry to deprive you of your moral superiority.

Michel But Paul said . . .

Laurence He was lying!

Pause. She moves away. She seems terribly sad.

Michel What's the matter?

Laurence What's the matter? My husband tells me he's had a mistress for six months . . . Otherwise, everything's fine.

Michel But you as well, you . . .

Laurence No. *Not me!*

Pause.

Michel You mean . . . What do you . . . I don't understand what any of you are saying!

Laurence If you'd felt the slightest bit of love for me, if you'd had the slightest regard for my feelings, you'd have made sure I never found out. You'd have made sure I was protected.

Michel What are you talking about?

Laurence Your affair with Alice.

Michel What? What affair? I never had an affair with Alice.

Laurence You just told me you did.

Michel It was an expression . . . A metaphor . . . It was . . .

Laurence Stop it, Michel.

Pause.

Do you love her?

Michel Of course not!

Laurence You didn't even love her?

Michel No.

Laurence Then why?

Michel I don't know.

Laurence You've been lying to me for months . . . You've been lying to your best friend . . . You've been lying to everyone.

Michel Today I'm telling you the truth.

Laurence Yes, but by accident. And that's exactly why I'm blaming you. I'm not naive . . . I know very well you can't force someone to be faithful for twenty years . . . But at least you can ask him to be discreet. I would never have done something like this.

Michel You'd have lied to me?

Laurence Certainly.

Michel I thought you knew . . . That's why I waded straight in . . . I'm sorry. If you knew how much I love you.

Laurence Easy to say.

Michel Yes, but it's true. I mean . . . I'm here. In front of you. You're there. We love each other. Have done for twenty years . . . After all, that is something.

Pause.

I promise you, as of today, I'll be a better liar. I'll lie to you whenever necessary.

Laurence (*ironically*) Promise?

Michel (*astonished by what's happening*) Yes.

Laurence And I promise you that I'll lie to you in return.

Michel (*frowning*) Thank you.

Laurence Think nothing of it.

Pause.

Where did you see her?

Michel What?

Laurence Alice . . . How did it work?

Michel What's it matter?

Laurence Tell me.

Michel I thought you preferred not to know anything.

Laurence Too late now. Now you've told me, I need to know. I have to know the whole truth. Understand? If not, I don't see how we can go on living together . . .

Michel You want me to tell you 'the whole truth'?

Laurence Yes. The whole truth.

Michel (*embarrassed*) Ah.

Laurence Well? How did it work?

Michel Mm? We arranged meetings.

Laurence Where?

Michel Mm? In hotels. Not very often . . . Very rarely.

Laurence Hotels?

Michel (*starting to lie again*) Yes. Hotel *bars*. For tea. We spent a bit of time together.

Laurence And Paul found out?

Michel Yes and no. You know, there wasn't much to find out . . . I mean it wasn't an affair . . . Not in the classic sense of the word. We saw each other once or twice. No more than that . . .

Laurence You told me it lasted six months.

Michel No, no . . . It started six months ago . . . And stopped very soon after . . . I mean . . . We hardly even kissed . . . You know, we were in an impossible situation . . . If you really want to know everything, 'the whole truth', I think if she hadn't been Paul's wife, it might have gone a little further. I mean, maybe, it's possible. I mean, something stronger. But it wasn't possible. Given the situation. With Paul.

Laurence Do you still see her?

Michel What? No. Of course not. I told you, it's in the past. Anyway, I think Paul's going to live in Sweden.

Laurence (*reacting*) What?

Michel Yes.

Laurence What are you talking about?

Michel So he just told me . . . He got an answer today. They've offered him a job over there.

Laurence But I thought his interview was for a job in Paris . . .

Michel Yes. To start with, yes. Then finally they offered him this other thing. Finance director. In Stockholm.

Laurence And is he going to accept?

Michel That's what he told me.

Laurence (*worried*) Are you sure?

Michel He just told me.

Pause. She moves away. This news seems to have made an unexpected impact on her.

Michel I imagine Alice will go with him . . . I won't see her any more. I'm telling you this to reassure you. But in any case, we'd taken the decision not to see each other any more. We took the decision some time ago. It just wasn't possible. I don't know how other men behave, but for me, it's beyond my abilities . . . I can't split myself in two. Deception is beyond me . . . That's probably what I was looking for in her, to confirm to myself that I wasn't that kind of man . . .

She seems to be elsewhere. Is she thinking about Paul?

Are you listening?

Laurence What?

Michel What are you thinking about?

Laurence Nothing. Nothing at all.

She seems to be rising above some sadness, a sadness connected to the departure of Paul.

Laurence (*abruptly*) Do you love me?

Michel Are you crying?

Laurence Do you love me?

Michel More than ever. I feel terribly guilty, you know. If you knew, darling, how guilty I feel for causing you so much pain . . . Please, wipe your eyes . . . Don't be sad. Now it's all out in the open, now we've told each other

84

'the whole truth', however painful it is, we can go out, can't we? Providing you've forgiven me . . . I promise you, this was all for the good. From now on, everything's going to be fine. Now there are no more shadows between us.

Laurence Yes.

Michel We can start again. My darling . . . On a firm footing.

Laurence No lies.

Michel No lies, that's right . . . The truth and nothing but the truth.

They hold each other tight, relieved at having sidestepped the truth one more time. Michel kisses her on the forehead, trying to console a sadness he can't understand.

Blackout.